Wheatgrass Juice
Gift of Nature

or

The Natural High

By: Betsy Russell Manning

The Family Tree of Grasses

Give me the splendid silent sun
with all his beams full-dazzling,
Give me juicy autumnal fruit
ripe and red from the orchard,
Give me a field where the unmow'd grass grows,
the good green grass, that delicate miracle,
The ever-recurring grass . . .

— Walt Whitman

This booklet is lovingly dedicated to
my son, Kevin Patrick Manning

With special thanks to
Viktoras Kulvinskas,
Zak Mohammed, John Morphy
and Diane Daria

Artist . . . . . Kim Arnold

I would like to take this opportunity to thank most sincerely the authors of the books I have researched. Please note Reference Section.

Contents

Betsy at Hippocrates-West Wheatgrass Cathedral. 1981
San Diego

Raychel Solomon, Director of Hippocrates-West showing the organic garden harvest.

Christmas 1980
San Diego

History of Wheat

WHEATBERRIES ARE THE SEEDS USED FOR WHEATGRASS

Wheatberries are the whole wheat kernel which has only the chaff and straw removed.

WHEATBERRY IN ANCIENT TIMES

In ancient times, the wheatberry was considered to be the most valuable of foods. Likewise, the *chlorophyll* from the growing wheat has proven itself for cleansing the bloodstream. *Wheatgrass,* freshly made into a drink, contains liquid sunshine plus the electric current necessary to revitalize the body.

After a time of approximately 3,000 years, wheat was found by Lord Carnavon in the tomb of the Egyptian King, Tutankhamen. The wheat was planted in France (1923) and grew magnificently.

WHEAT AND CEREALS IN THE YEAR 2800 B.C.

Cereals, including wheat, were used by the Greeks as a gift from Demeter, the goddess of agriculture, and by the Romans as a credit to Goddess Ceres. As early as 2800 B.C. elaborate ceremonies were conducted in China honoring the cereals.

Wheatgrass was used in ancient China and, I understand, still is, as a tonic in the spring and as a blood purifier.

It seems wheat has been grown prior to, or at least since, recorded history. Nearly one-half of the cultivated land on the planet is used for cereal production and one-third of it is used for wheat production.

All cereals in their natural state, especially where the dark outer layers of wheat, barley, rye and rice are retained, make perfect food.

STORING WHEATBERRIES FOR THEIR HIGH NUTRITIONAL VALUE

Wheat is one of the finest grains to store for survival because it is so high in nutritional value.* Wheat picks up 92 of the 102 minerals in the soil. It contains calcium, phosphorus, magnesium, sodium and potassium. *Wheatgrass,* the article continues, is a complete food. It is high in protein which the pancreas needs to aid digestion of starches. Because of its *chlorophyll* content, wheatgrass is one of the finest blood builders and body rejuvenators.

**Health Magic Through Chlorophyll From Living Plant Life*

HOW TO STORE WHEATBERRIES

Keep in tightly covered container in cool, dry, dark place.

SURVIVE WITH WHEATGRASS

In a disaster or national emergency *wheatgrass* would be a readily available food supply.

A curse was placed upon King Nebuchadnezzar (in the Book of Daniel). He became physically and mentally ill. He was advised by Heaven to "eat grass as did the oxen." Upon following this advice he made a complete recovery.

NUTRITIVE VALUE OF WHEATGRASS

Wheatgrass is one of the richest natural sources of vitamin A and vitamin C. Wheatgrass has all known minerals. However, this is limited by the quality of soil and seed.

Sprague, Crampton and Harris through separate studies bring out that *wheatgrass* is an excellent source of calcium, iron, magnesium, phosphorus, potassium, sodium, sulphur, cobalt, and zinc.

Dr. Burkholder of Yale states that grasses are exceptionally rich in B vitamins.

ANTIBIOTIC PROPERTIES OF THE WHEAT SEED

Wheat contains antibiotic properties active against Gram-positive bacteria and fungi when tested in vitro, according to Peter Ark, Professor Emeritus of Plant Pathology, University of California, Berkeley.

*Wheatgrass is One of the Highest Sources of *Chlorophyll*

Chlorophyll** = **Wheatgrass Juice

The solid content of juice made from *wheatgrass* is 70 percent *chlorophyll.*

Dr. George Crile, M.D. stated at a medical convention that in the future man will try to get the sunshine element from the plant to rejuvenate the human body.**

Wheatgrass juice is a crude *chlorophyll* and can be taken orally or as an implant without worry of toxic side effects.

Chlorophyll is often referred to as "the blood of plant life." It closely resembles the molecules of human red blood cells.

Chlorophyll is the basis of all plant life.

***Health Magic Through Chlorophyll From Living Plant Life*

Chlorophyll is liquid sunshine.

Chlorophyll is one of nature's greatest healers for conditions inside and outside the body.

Chlorophyll is a survival food because it feeds us dynamic nutrients, yet the body gives up little energy to get these nutrients.

Chlorophyll absorbs energy from the sun and in some unknown way uses it for the manufacture of sugar, starch and proteins.

Science has proven not only that *chlorophyll* will arrest growth and development of unfriendly bacteria, but is actually akin to human blood.

Chlorophyll has the same chemical structure as hemoglobin (red cells in human blood), according to studies done in 1911.

Both *chlorophyll* (wheatgrass) and hemoglobin consist in part of similar atoms. The only actual difference between the two is that in human blood the metallic atom or element of the hemoglobin consists of iron, while in chlorophyll this atom is magnesium.

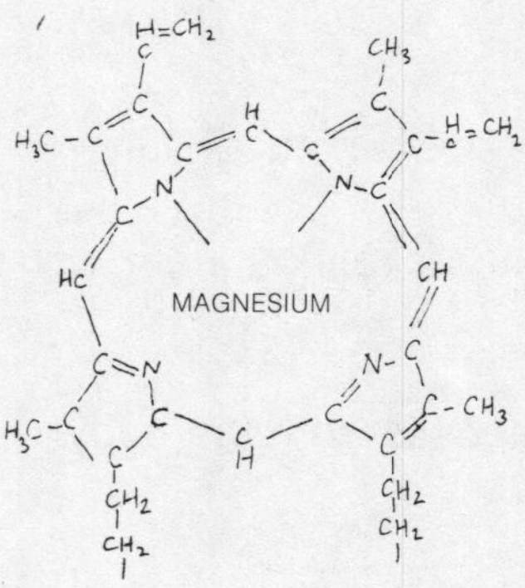

CHLOROPHYLL MOLECULE

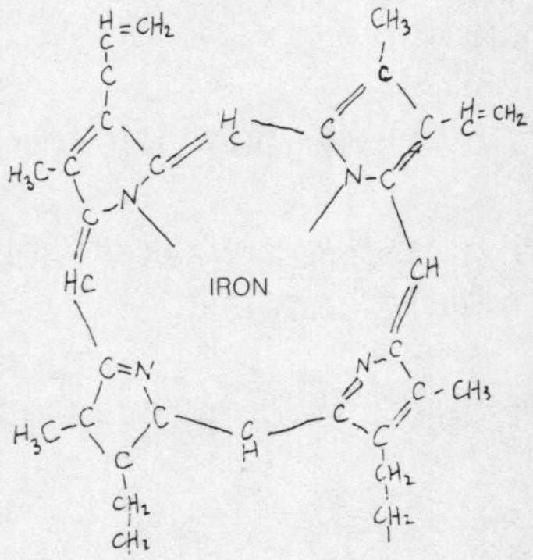

HEMIN BLOOD MOLECULE

Chlorophyll (wheatgrass) aids in rebuilding the bloodstream. Studies on various animals have shown chlorophyll to be free of any toxic reaction. The red cell count was returned to normal within 4 to 5 days of the administration of chlorophyll, even in those animals which were known to be extremely anemic or low in red cell count.

Extensive laboratory investigation has shown that tissue cell activity and its normal regrowth are definitely increased by the administration of *chlorophyll* (wheatgrass).

Chlorophyll (wheatgrass) in liquid form, as well as in ointment or powder form, possesses remarkable properties when used in treatments of chronically infected or ulcerated wounds. It has a retarding action upon the bacteria which contaminates such infections.

Chlorophyll (wheatgrass) acts to produce an unfavorable environment for bacterial growth, rather than by any direct action upon the bacteria themselves.

Chlorophyll juice may be extracted from many plants. However, *wheatgrass* has been chosen over other greens because it has all the ingredients desirable for health.

Chlorophyll has proven very effective in all chronic disorders.

Chlorophyll goes into the red blood cells immediately.

Liquid *chlorophyll* gets into the tissues, refines them, and makes them over.

Liquid *chlorophyll* washes drug deposits from the body.

Chlorophyll helps counteract toxins which have been ingested.

Chlorophyll helps purify the liver.

Chlorophyll improves blood sugar problems.

Chlorophyll helps sores heal faster.

Dr. Chiu-Nan Lai, Ph.D., of the University of Texas System Cancer Center, Department of Biology, Houston, Texas has determined through using the Ames Bacterial Mutagenicity Test that *Chlorophyll* is the active factor in wheat sprout extract which inhibits the metabolic activiation of carcinogens.*

Chlorophyll was praised in the 1940 American Journal of Surgery by Benjamin Gruskin, M.D. for its antiseptic benefits. The article recommends the following clinical uses for *Chlorophyll* to clear up foul-smelling odors,neutralize strep infections, heal wounds, hasten skin grafting, cure chronic sinusitis, overcome chronic inner ear inflammation and infection, reduce varicose veins and heal leg ulcers, eliminate impetigo and other scabby eruptions, heal rectal sores, successfully treat inflammation of the uterine cervix, get rid of parasitic vaginal infections, reduce typhoid fever, and cure advanced pyorrhea in many cases.

Nutritionist Bernard Jensen lauds the virtues of *Chlorophyll* because of the magnetic and electrical quality of the raw enzymes it contains. It takes hours of energy to digest solid food, he maintains, but only minutes and very little energy for the body to assimilate *Chlorophyll*.

**(This commonly used short-term test is frequently utilized by regulatory-environmental agencies and cancer research for the screening of potential carcinogens). The Ames Test was formulated by Dr. Bruce Ames, Professor and Chairman, Dept. of Biochemistry, Univ. of California, Berkeley.*

Uses of Wheatgrass Juice

Wheatgrass juice purifies the blood.

Wheatgrass juice acts as a detergent in the body.

Use *wheatgrass* juice for dandruff, rub the juice into the scalp. Rinse and shampoo.

Use *wheatgrass* juice for vaginal infection. Put wheatgrass juice in syringe and squirt into the vaginal area.

Douche with *wheatgrass* juice.

ORAL USES OF WHEATGRASS

A small amount of *wheatgrass* in the human diet prevents tooth decay. Tooth decay is the result of other degenerative changes in the body.

Gargle with *wheatgrass* juice for toothaches.

Gargle with *wheatgrass* juice for a sore throat.

Pyorrhea of the mouth: Take pulp or *wheatgrass* (soaked in juice), lay in mouth on diseased area or chew *wheatgrass* in mouth (spitting out the pulp).

WHEATGRASS JUICE FOR OTHER USES

Drink *wheatgrass* juice for skin troubles: eczema, psoriasis.

Wheatgrass juice can be used as a sterilizer.

Wheatgrass juice keeps the hair from greying.

Use *wheatgrass* juice as a source of fresh, alive vitamins!

Use *wheatgrass* as a protective and healing power.

Taking *wheatgrass* juice we will feel the difference in our sense of strength, health, spirituality, endurance and well being.

Wheatgrass juice will help to build a clean bloodstream and aid in proper digestion. It is also an excellent mouthwash and draws out toxins from the gums and teeth.

Wheatgrass juice is great for blood disorders of all kinds, including anemia.

Wheatgrass juice is high in enzymes.

Wheatgrass juice is an excellent skin cleanser and can be absorbed through the skin for nutrition. Pour green juice over you in tub of warm water. Soak in wheatgrass juice 15 to 20 minutes. Rinse off with cold shower.

Wheatgrass implants (enemas) are great for healing and detoxifying the colon walls. The implants also heal and cleanse the internal organs. After an enema (wait 20 minutes) follow with 4 ounces grass juice (implant) and retain for 20 minutes.

Wheatgrass juice is excellent in a case of constipation, and keeping bowels open.

Wheatgrass juice disinfects and cleans out bacteria.

Dr. Birscher, a research scientist, called *chlorophyll* "concentrated sun power." He said, "Chlorophyll increases the function of the heart, affects the vascular system, the intestines, the uterus, and the lungs."*

According to Dr. Birscher, nature uses *chlorophyll* (wheatgrass) as a body cleanser, rebuilder and neutralizer of toxins.

Wheatgrass juice can dissolve the scars that are formed in the lungs from breathing acid gasses. The effect of carbon monoxide is minimized, since *chlorophyll* increases hemoglobin production.

Wheatgrass juice reduces high blood pressure as the juice helps remove toxins from the body and gives the blood iron which helps circulation.

Wheatgrass enhances the capillaries.

Guanidine, a toxic substance, released through trauma and burns causes muscle fatigue, putrification, headaches and stomach aches. *Wheatgrass* juice neutralizes guanidine.

Wheatgrass juice is excellent for sex hormones, as the juice contains vitamin E.

* *Garden Indoors*

WHEATGRASS AND RADIATION

Many tests are being made which point to a *chlorophyll* (wheatgrass) rich diet affecting the survival of experimental animals undergoing lethal doses of radiation.* In 1950, Lourau and Lartigue reported that cabbage supplement (chlorophyll) increases the resistance of guinea pigs to radiation.

X-RAYS

If you have had an X-ray recently, or live in the city, a glass of green juice taken daily on an indefinite basis will greatly slow down harmful effects.

The solid content of juice made from *wheatgrass* is 70% *chlorophyll.* The enzyme content is at its maximum at this stage. Like most whole foods it is rich in laetrile (B-17) which can selectively destroy cancer cells, but has little effect on normal cells. According to Dr. Krebs, the laetrile content in sprouts and young fresh greens increases up to 100 times beyond that of the seeds from which they originated.**

Television, especially colored, gives off radiation. Put some green plants or *wheatgrass* in front of the T.V., and it will absorb radiation. Also wheatgrass or green plants will absorb pollution and odors in your home.

Suggested reading on radiation:

Are You Radioactive? Linda Clark Pyramid Press
Health and Light John Ott Pocket Press

**Radiation Reports* (See Pages 20 - 22)
***Survival is Possible*

WHEATGRASS AND ANIMALS

Animals have been observed to choose, during periods of illness, a diet consisting almost exclusively of green vegetation.

HOW TO MAKE A POULTICE OF WHEATGRASS

Juice the *wheatgrass,* preferably with a wheatgrass juicer. Soak pulp in juice. Gather pulp in plastic bag, put cloth over it and tape on to the wound or sore for healing.

Use *wheatgrass* poultice for sores and boils, burns, cuts and insect bites.

WHEATGRASS FOR TRAVELLING

Chew a handful of *wheatgrass* for the juice. Spit out the pulp. When travelling a long distance by car, chew on wheatgrass and your energy level will stay high.

HOW MUCH WHEATGRASS JUICE TO TAKE

Wheatgrass, a great body builder, is a complete food and is very rich in *chlorophyll.* Start with one ounce a day and add a small amount of water. As you become accustomed to the wheatgrass, drop the water and work up to 6 ounces of wheatgrass juice a day. Your energy level will be very high.

Wheatgrass juice should be mixed thoroughly with your saliva before swallowing. Drink very slowly.

Drink *wheatgrass* one hour before meals and two hours after meals.

Wheatgrass juice is a powerful cleanser and may cause nausea, thus starting an immediate reaction with toxins and mucus in the stomach.

WHEATGRASS AND TOXICITY

Toxicity studies have shown that *chlorophyll* is absolutely non-toxic when administered orally or intravenously to animals and humans. Studies on various animals have shown chlorophyll to be free of any toxic reaction.

WHEATGRASS AND WATER

A few blades of *wheatgrass* were added to fluoridated water for several minutes. When the grass was later removed and the water tested, no fluorine was detected. Later, an official from the water department of New York City tested some fluoridated water to which wheatgrass had been added with the same results. Wheatgrass makes harmful inorganic chemicals harmless.

WHEATGRASS, FRUITS AND VEGETABLES

Fruits and vegetables contaminated by sprays can be cleaned with a few blades of *wheatgrass* placed in the rinse water.

According to Dr. Earp-Thomas, 15 pounds of fresh *wheatgrass* is equivalent in nutritional value to 350 pounds of the choicest vegetables.

WHEATGRASS JUICE IN PREGNANCY

Start with one teaspoon of *wheatgrass* juice in some water and work up to what feels comfortable. This will be a good supplement because it contains almost every element needed for nourishment.

WHEATGRASS JUICE AND BABIES

For babies one year and older, start out by putting one teaspoon of *wheatgrass* juice in spring water. Gradually increase.

WHEATGRASS JUICE FOR THE HYPERACTIVE CHILD

Dr. Elizabeth Rees, M.D., lecturer at the Association for Children with Learning Disabilities — International Conference, San Francisco (February - March 1979), states that lead, mercury and cadmium are all heavy metal poisons that damage the nervous system and affect the liver and kidneys.

Dr. Rees goes on to say, "Since the rise of the Industrial Revolution we have been breathing in *tetraethyl lead* used in our gasoline. We breathe in 90% of this lead as it is absorbed through the lungs."

According to Dr. Rees, "There are studies showing that the percentage of children with lead poisoning among hyperactive children is far far higher than it is among the children who are behaving themselves."

HOW TO USE WHEATGRASS TO REMOVE TOXIC METALS FROM CHILDREN

Lead, cadmium, mercury, aluminum and excessive copper (we need a small amount of copper) can be successfully lowered with small amounts of *wheatgrass* juice, increased gradually.

Start out with one ounce daily in a small amount of water, or apple juice and water, or lime and water, or lemon and water.

Wheatgrass will also bring up the level of calcium, iron, magnesium, phosphorus, potassium, sodium, sulphur, etc. in the child.

★ ★ ★

The following page shows a hair analysis report of a child who had a high level of toxic metals (lead, etc.) in his system and an over-supply of copper.

However, after drinking *wheatgrass* juice for two months the copper level appeared normal and the toxic metals were shown to be lower.

Dr. Ann Wigmore and Raychel Solomon speaking at dedication of Hippocrates — West.

San Diego
June 1979

HAIR ANALYSIS REPORT

BATCH - SAMPLE	[illegible]
CONTROL NO.	
DATE REC'D.	03/19/79
DATE COMPLETED	03/21/79

PERSONAL INFORMATION

NAME.

Sex		Hair Location	HEAD
Age		Hair Color, NATURAL	
Ht.	' "	Hair Coloring	
Wt.		Shampoo	
Race		Occupation	

SIGNIFICANT RATIOS

MINERALS	VALUE	MIDLINE IDEAL
Ca: Mg	10.0	8:1
Ca: Mn	330.	80:1
Ca: Zn	0.71	2:1
Na: K	1.8	2:1
Fe: Cu	0.93	1.5:1
Zn: Cu	10.0	8:1
Zn: Mn	470.	40:1
Zn: Cd	330.	2000:1
Zn: Pb	14.0	200:1

RETURN TO ADDRESS

COMPLAINTS:

NOTE: ALL MINERALS REPORTED IN mg%
(1 mg% = 10 ppm)

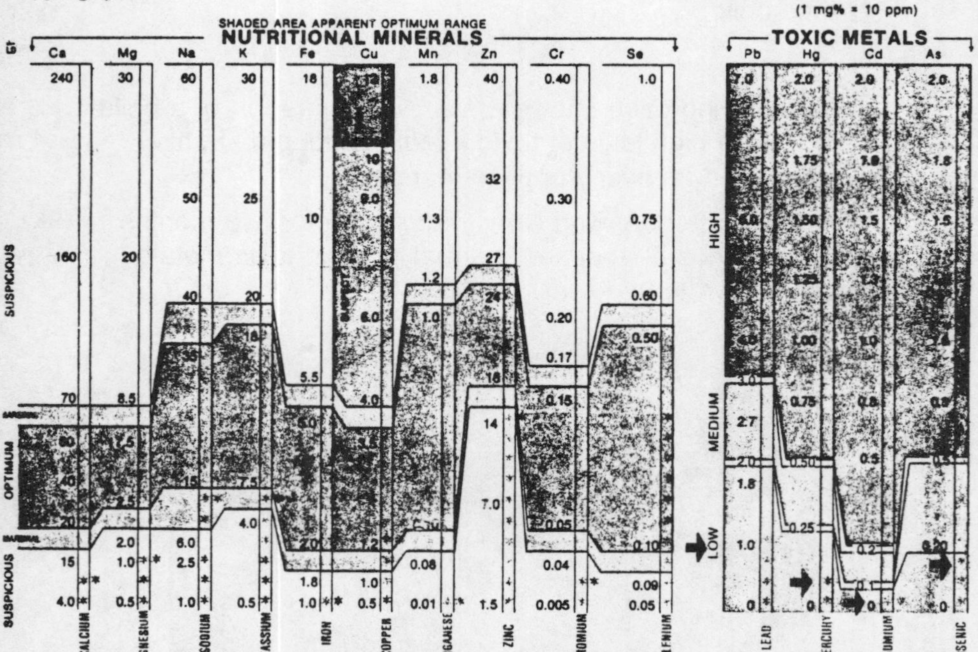

Ca	Mg	Na	K	Fe	Cu	Mn	Zn	Cr	Se	Pb	Hg	Cd	As
10.	1.00	11.	6.2	1.3	1.4	.030	14.	0.030	0.33	1.00	.070	.043	0.16

ADDITIONAL MINERALS

MINERAL	MG%	RANGE
AL	0.43	0.2-1.0
LI	0.008	<0.20
NI	0.027	0.03-0.10
CO	0.014	<0.10
P	17.	10-17
MO	0.077	0.01-0.07

***NOTE:** Arrows indicate low toxic metal levels (after taking wheatgrass juice for several months).

GREEN DRINKS

Eydie Mae's Green Drink

2 oz. wheatgrass juice
2 oz. Rejuvelac*

Wheatgrass - Pineapple Juice

1 oz. wheatgrass juice
1 oz. pineapple juice

Mixed Vegetable Juice

4 oz. carrot juice
2 oz. celery juice
1 oz. beet juice
1-8 oz. wheatgrass juice
parsley
kelp
tomato

Wheatgrass - Carrot Juice Drink

1 oz. wheatgrass
3 oz. carrot juice

Linda's Cocktail

1 or more ounces of wheatgrass juice
1 lemon or lime, juiced
6 oz. distilled water
mint oil or
fresh mineral water

Betsy's Alfalfa-Green Drink

4 oz. wheatgrass juice
juice one small salad bowl of alfalfa sprouts

* To make Rejuvelac use 3 cups distilled water to 1 cup soft spring wheat (organic). Let stand first time 48 hours in room temperature. Pour soak water out and refill again with 3 cups distilled water. Let stand second time 24 hours. Pour soak water into jar and use as fermented drink. Use same seeds once again with 3 cups water and pour off second time in 24 hours. Cover jar loosely, allowing air to enter. Rejuvelac contains many B vitamins. Rinse seeds before you begin. **(See Page 19 for address of soft-spring wheat)**

Betsy with Eydie Mae, author of *How I Conquered Cancer Naturally.*
San Diego, January 1979

HOW TO GROW INDOOR GREENS (WHEATGRASS, ETC.)

Reprinted with permission: *Holistic H.E.L.P. Handbook* by Stan Kalson.
P.O. Box 15103, Phoenix, Ariz. 85060

Equipment

A cafeteria tray or pie plate, hard red winter wheat, sunflower and buckwheat seed, soil (best organic soil available) to fill tray to the top, 8-10 layers of newspaper, 1 sheet of plastic to cover top of tray, or an identical tray to use in place of plastic or newspaper, and water.

Method

1 Soak seed in water 12 hours. If using pie plate soak approximately 1/2 cup of dry seed; the amount of seed depends upon size of tray. (12" x 16" cafeteria tray holds 1 cup of seed.) Pour off water, and allow soaked seeds to drain for 12 hours.

2 Place soil onto tray and level with hand for smooth surface.

3 Wet soil. Use fine spray. DO NOT SOAK.

4 Place soaked seeds on top of wet soil and gingerly spread out seeds on soil so that seeds are side by side but 1 seed thick only.

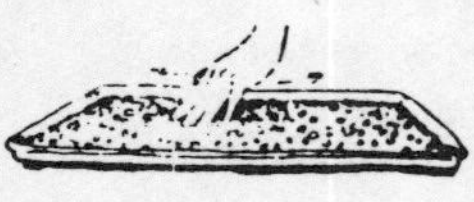

5 Soak newspaper throughout. Cut newspaper to exact size of tray and cover seed.

6 Place plastic on top of soaked newspaper (cut exactly to size of tray). Optional: (or cover with tray that is exact size. Be aware that in extremely dry climates the wet newspaper and plastic are more effective. Experiment with both methods and choose what works best for you.)

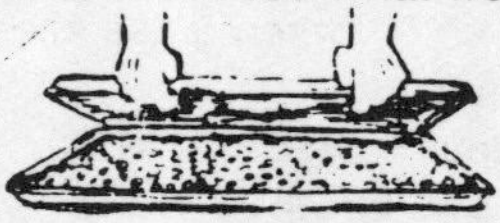

7 Find place where covered trays can sit for 3 days. Ventilation important-room not too warm.

8 After 3 days, take paper (or top trays) off trays; water each day if necessary. Mist greens in dry weather conditions.

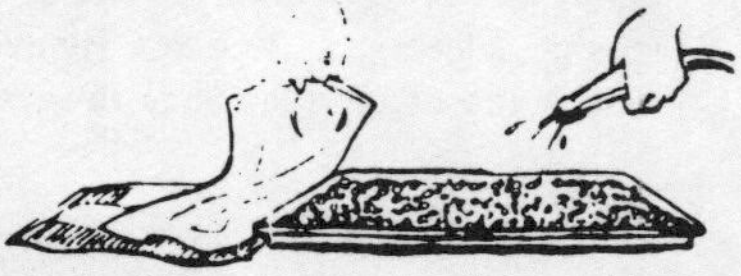

9 Next, take trays to a lighted area. Water once each day if necessary; DO NOT SOAK SOIL.

10 When greens are approximately 6"-8" high and standing tall with a lush green color they are ready to cut. About 5 additional days.

11 Cut greens close to soil with a sharp knife. They are ready for use. Greens can be stored in refrigerator in plastic bags.

MACHINES FOR JUICING WHEATGRASS

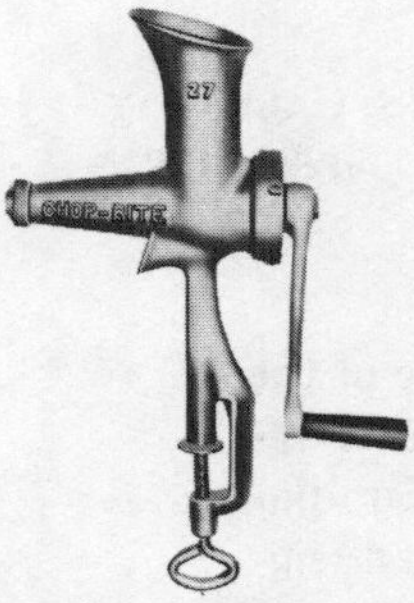

Hand Juicer

Electric Juicer

The juice should be extracted either by chewing or utilizing a slow action machine as seen above.

Grasses can be grown year round in any apartment or house, city or country. *Wheatgrass* is alive and feeds oxygen to your body.

WHAT KIND OF SEED TO USE FOR PLANTING

Use only organic seed. The seed used for planting is called "hard-red winter wheat."
Look for organic wheat in your health food store; or write to Arrowhead Mills, Inc., for an outlet in your area. (P.O. Box 2059, Hereford, Texas 79045; ph. 806 364-0730)

WHEATGRASS AND EARTHWORMS

The earthworm is a major influence on the health of every human being on this planet. So important are the activities of earthworms that any soil-building program in your outside garden can only be partially successful unless you make provision for their presence. These little fellows are nature's workers in soil rejuvenation. They actually till the soil around the roots of plants, their burrows forming tunnels through which the rootlets are allowed to spread, to receive needed oxygen from the air and moisture from the rain.

Reduction of X-Radiation Mortality by Cabbage and Broccoli.*

HARRY SPECTOR AND DORIS HOWES CALLOWAY
U. S. Army QM Food and Container Inst. for Armed Forces, QMR & E C
Chicago

In studying composition of diet as one of the factors contributing to large variation in resistance of guinea pigs to whole body X-radiation, Lourau and Lartigue(1) reported significantly higher mortality and incidence of hemorrhages in animals receiving supplement of beets, than in those receiving supplement of cabbage. (An unsupplemented control group was not available.) They considered 2 possible explanations: cabbage is protective and diminishes incidence of hemorrhages because of high content of Vit. P and C; or, beets contain a substance perfectly tolerated by normal animal, but which becomes toxic to an irradiated animal. They adopted the latter explanation. This observation led us to perform experiments to test these reported effects of cabbage and beets and to investigate ability of other foods to increase or decrease mortality due to radiation exposure.

Materials and methods. Young male albino guinea pigs, weighing 250 to 325 g, were maintained on basal diet of equal parts of whole field oats and wheat bran, *ad lib.* Supplements of beets (75 g), cabbage (50 g) or broccoli (50 g) were given to at least 2 groups of animals. Raw vegetables were diced and given in separate cups.† Lyophilized cabbage was wetted with twice its weight of distilled water. After 2 weeks of pre-feeding, all animals were exposed to 400 r of whole-body X-radiation. Irradiation was carried out at Argonne National Laboratory‡ using a General Electric Maximar X-ray machine. Radiation factors were 180 KV, 15 ma, no filtration

*Reproduced copy of Radiation Report

added, 21-22 r/minute, 41 inches target distance. Six animals were irradiated simultaneously in horizontal beam and each exposure included representatives from each group. Half of the dose was applied to each side of animals.

Results. One hundred percent of 94 guinea pigs fed only the basal diet died within 10 to 15 days after irradiation (Fig. 1). Supplementation with beets did not affect mortality rate of irradiated guinea pigs during the 30-day test. Feeding raw cabbage significantly reduced mortality in all 7 trials to average of 52% (range, 20 to 64%)§ Lyophilized cabbage was fed at level equivalent to 50 g of raw cabbage, and retained ability to reduce radiation mortality. Another member of the *Brassicaceae* family, *i.e.*, broccoli, was found in 2 trials to be even more effective than cabbage in reducing radiation mortality. Analysis of variance of proportions of animals killed during the 30-day test (using arc sine transformation) showed that the difference in mortality due to feeding of cabbage or broccoli, was highly significnt ($p < .001$) (2).

We then determined separate effects of pre- and post-irradiation feeding of cabbage. Significance of results was evaluated by analysis of variance of cumulative proportions of animals killed at each time period (using arc sine transformation) averaged over 30 days. Pre-feeding of guinea pigs with cabbage just prior to radiation exposure, significantly ($p < .001$) delayed onset of death and enabled some animals to survive the test period (Fig. 2). Post-irradiation supplementation with cabbage yielded significantly ($p < .001$) lower total mortality. The greatest number of survivors resulted from feeding of cabbage both before and after radiation exposure.

Average consumption of basal bran and oats diet was 14 g/day by control groups and by guinea pigs fed a vegetable supplement. Irradiation had a relatively small effect on food consumption. Intake of basal diet was about 60% of normal for first 4 days and gradually increased to pre-irradiation level by 21st day. Intake of cabbage dropped 3 to 5 g between 8th and 20th days. Body weight changes followed a typical pattern of initial loss on day 1, followed by gradual recovery until 8th-post-irradiation day, when a second period of weight loss occurred, persisting until 13th day. Representative changes in body weight are shown in Table I. Some mortality occurred at time of initial weight loss, the major incidence of death, however, was simultaneous with second period of weight loss, between 11th and 13th days. Animals which survive this second phase, in general, survive the 30-day test.

Protective effect of cabbage supplementation has also been demonstrated in another species, the rat (unpublished), maintained on standard synthetic ration which is nutritionally adequate in all known nutrients. Studies are in progress to explore these important findings by survey of wide variety of foods, which increase or decrease sensitivity of rats and guinea pigs to radiation injury and to ascertain whether these effects occur in other species of animals.‖

§ In exploratory trials ascorbic had no influence on mortality and was therefore included in drinking water of all animals at level of 75 mg/100 ml.

‖ Acknowledgement is made to the following for assistance in these experiments: Dr. Leonard Sheffner, Lucius Thomas, Gladys Eckfeldt and Robert Potts.

Summary. Exposure to 400 r of whole-body X-radiation resulted in 100% mortality in 10 to 15 days of young male guinea pigs fed a basal diet of bran and oats plus ascorbic acid. Supplementation with cabbage or broccoli for 2 weeks before irradiation and during 30 days after irradiation significantly reduced mortalty. Lyophilized cabbage retained ability to reduce radiation mortality. Pre-feeding of guinea pigs to time of radiation exposure, signficantly delayed onset of death and enabled some animals to survive test period. Post-irradiation supplementation with cabbage also yielded a lower total mortality. Feeding of cabbage both before and after radiation exposure produced greatest amount of protection.

1. Lourau, M., Lartigue, O., *Experientia,* 1950, v6 25.

2. Fisher-Yates Tables, 1953, Table XII, p66.

Received December 2, 1958. P.S.E.B.M., 1959, v100

NUTRITION & RADIATION INJURY

An Annotated Bibliography
By
Doris Howes Calloway

Former Chief, Nutrition Branch
U.S. Army QM Food and Container Inst. For
Armed Forces, QMR & E Command — Chicago

B. GREEN PLANT MATERIALS

CALLOWAY, D.H., A.H. MUNSON, & R. HILF.—QMFCIAF RPT. 37-60, 1960

Young male guinea pigs were fed a basal diet of bran and oats, with or without a daily exposure to 400 r.w.b. X-irradiation. Animals were killed sequentially for histologic and hematologic examination. Provision of broccoli resulted in improved nutrition, larger livers with higher stores of vitamin A and minimal fatty changes, and superior gonadal development. Following irradiation in both groups, decrements in body weight and food intake as well as the characteristic events of the radiation syndrome were seen. Broccoli supplementation of the cereal diet generally *reduced** the degree of distortion or delayed its appearance.

DUPLAN, J.F.—COMPT. REND. ACAD. SCI. PARIS, 236:424-26, 1953

Guinea pigs fed a basal diet of bran and oats together with green *cabbage** or carrots were exposed to 300, 500, or 1000 R of X-irradiation. Cabbage reduced mortality and body weight loss.

LOURAU, M. & O. LARTIGUE—EXPERIENTIA 6:25-26, 1949

Supplementation of a bran-oats diet with *cabbage** results in improved radioresistance in the guinea pig, as compared with a supplement of beets.

**Author's italics*

REFERENCES

U.S. Army QM Food and Containers Inst.
FOR ARMED FORCES, QMR & E Command,
Chicago, Ill., 1959 .... H. Spector & D. Calloway

Chlorophyll, Nature's "Green Magic" .... T.M. Rudolph, Ph.D.

Healthy Children .... Dr. Ann Wigmore

Be Your Own Doctor .... Dr. Ann Wigmore

Survival into the 21st Century .... Viktoras Kulvinskas

Nature's Healing Grasses .... H.E. Kirschner, M.D.

Organic Soil .... Dr. Earp-Thomas

Health Magic Through Chlorophyll
From Living Plant Life .... B. Jensen

How I Conquered Cancer Naturally .... Eydie Mae Hunsberger

Survival is Possible When You Work with Nature .... Dr. Ann Wigmore

Garden Indoors .... Dr. Ann Wigmore

Comfrey and Chlorophyll .... Vincent Licata

Mutation Research, 77:245-50, 1980 ....Dr. Chiu Nan Lai, Ph.D.

Nutrition & Cancer, 1:1, 1978 & 1:3, 1979 .....Dr. Chiu Nan Lai, Ph.D.

Antibiotic Properties of the Seeds of Wheat & Barley
Vol.42, No.8–Plant Disease Reporter–Aug. 15, 1958
University of California, Berkeley ....Peter Ark, Ph.D.

Chlorophyll–Its theraputic place in acute and suppurative disease.
Vol. XLIX, No. 1, p. 49-55-American Journal of Surgery, 1940
.... Benjamin Gruskin, M.D.

The Treatment of Cancer with Herbs, Bio-World Pub. 1984, p. 152-153
........................John Heinerman, Master Herbologist, Ph.D.

Viktoras Kulvinskas and LifeLighter Friends behind Wheatgrass Booth at the National Health Federation Convention.

January 1981
Long Beach

Linda behind the Wheatgrass Booth at the Haight-Ashbury Fair.
May 1979

Betsy, with son, Kevin, and Linda at the Civic Center Plaza behind the "Wheatgrass Juice Stand," for the "Stop Diablo Canyon Nuclear Power Plant — Rally & Energy Fair."

April 7, 1979
San Francisco

Betsy at Doheny State Beach Park for "Coalition to Stop San Onofre."

November 10, 1979
Dana Point

Order Form

Betsy Russell-Manning
c/o Greensward Press
1600 Larkin #104
San Francisco, Ca. 94109
(415) 928-4142

or

Cancer Control Society
2043 No. Berendo Street
Los Angeles, California 90027
(213) 663-7801

PLEASE SEND ME THE FOLLOWING BOOKS EDITED BY BETSY RUSSELL-MANNING

____copies CANDIDA, SILVER (MERCURY) FILLINGS AND THE IMMUNE SYSTEM at $15.95 each + $3.00 shipping (UPS)

____copies How SAFE ARE SILVER (MERCURY) FILLINGS?-HIDDEN HEALTH FACTS at $39.95 each + $3.00 shipping (UPS)

____copies WHEAT GRASS JUICE-GIFT OF NATURE at $2.95 each + $1.00; shipping (UPS)

____copies HOW SILVER MERCURY FILLINGS AFFECT YOUR ENERGY SYSTEM at $10.00 each + $1.50 shipping (UPS)

NAME ______________________________

STREET ______________________________

CITY ______________________________

NOTE: Californians please add 6½% Sales Tax.
Please add $1.00 extra for shipping 2nd book.
I can't wait for U.P.S. delivery. Here is $12.50 for next day air delivery.